# WOOLGATHERING

Dia



Typeset and Published by
The National Poetry Foundation
(Registered Charity No 283032)
27 Mill Road
Fareham
Hants PO16 0TH
(Tel/Fax 01329 822218)

Best wishes Ann
from Diana
Madingley July 2004.

Printed by
Consort Print Services
Consort Court, High Street
Fareham, Hants PO16 7AL
(Tel 01329 822530)

Sponsored by Rosemary Arthur

Edited by Johnathon Clifford

Poems previously published in: *Pause, The PHRAS Competition Winners' Anthology 1994, The Guernsey Evening Press* and by Ver Poets in 1997.



ISBN 1 900726 61 0

CONTENTS

**For John**

## TOMORROW FOILED

Today,
For jam we toiled.
We stripped the orchard bare
Of plum and quince, of apple and of pear,
Then boiled.

## SIESTA FOR ANT

The cracked stone waits for shade.
Crunch-dried leaves lie unstirred in
breezeless lavender-laden air
and Ant, starting, stopping, darting,
circles the careless crumb.
Tables turned, chairs askew,
scraps from a meal, long digested,
feed some flies while buzzing wasps
attack a rotting plum.
Wine dregs, blood-black, spoil a glass.
Behind closed shutters lovers sigh
uncovered on white sheets
and Ant pulls the prized crumb,
ten times his size,
backwards across the patio.

## AN AUTUMN BREAK

It’s no use sitting contemplating
the dark underbellies of shifting clouds
against a sea of blue sky,
or the world’s grey-green ocean
absorbing their dark shadows.
As husband trudges tall
around a November Cornwall
in his dubbined leather boots,
leaving half a duvet empty,
young daughters, giggling, bring
breakfast to my bed.
Spilt milk and tepid tea.
I must get up.
A patch of sun is caught
in the swirling froth of the bay
but there are things to be done!

## THE REDUNDANT YARD

*(Essex 1989)*

Crunching gravel greets the way into the old yard
where the barn, like a giant cracking egg-shell,
sheds its tiles and empty-bellied diesel tanks perch
on stilts of crumbling brick; mocking sentinel.

Rustling grasses swathe a rusting ploughshare.
Daisies push through asphalt cracks.
Oak saplings sprout between cobbles,
while bind-weed consumes some rotting hessian sacks.

The deserted workshop still smells of the grease and
iron filings imbedded in its packed earth floor,
while a leaning lean-to shelters a blacksmith's stove
with broken bellows; a remnant of a time before.

Drying barley, plump golden wheat and bouncing,
silky-black  rapeseed no longer fills the grainstore.
Instead, frightened birds fly from the rafters with
each flap and bang of the huge hanging door.

Silence muffles the engines, the clank of steel on
steel until a voice from the past wails and grieves
as the wind plays tricks with some wires and a ghost-
lorry gusts through on whirl of dead leaves.

No spring onions lie boxed and waiting in the rain,
nor lettuces, crisp and fresh from a dewy field.
Just empty crates, broken pallets, discarded trays,
and abandonment as an era is stealthily concealed.

## MULTILINGUAL PLAYGROUND

She watches the ball bounce,
one finger at her lip,
and hangs back, waiting,
hoping for acceptance.

Ball bouncing.
Bouncing ball.
*Hello! Hi There!*
*Bonjour! Ciao!*

Her eyes reel in the catch
hooked on an imagined elastic line
until someone calls out
"Fetch the bleedin' ball!"
and the line breaks.

With finger still damp,
she sprints to clutch the prize
then comes back triumphant,
happiness flooding her face.

## MY CHAMELEON SKIN

Skin beneath the cloth
changes with the mood
with each new situation.

Morning dress of jeans
sweatshirt, old leather shoes
to drive the kids to school
holding back potted anger
ready to scream.

Change at ten to ten
to smart skirt, tights
and coffee-morning blouse
with nip of brandy before
small talk begins.

Light suit for lecture-
lunch with the others
dressed accordingly
in business suits and ties
and polished shoes.

Now home to change,
as school run looms,
it's leggings and jumper
and jacket for the rain.
Kids home again.

Evening brings out the *Lycra* shorts,
worn *Asics* full of holes,
for running with the 'Girls'.
New club sweatshirt
for after drinks with new *Nikes*.

*Tomorrow I'll try*
*my new brown boots*
*and pleated woollen skirt.*
*Must feel the part*
*for flower arranging!*

## AFTERNOON BREAK IN THE INFANTS

Tim's staying in today, alone,
sent to sit in the book corner
for kicking Lucy Jones.
She came in crying this morning.

Her neat white tights holed,
blood oozing from her knee,
great tears sobbing down her mottled cheeks,
"Timmy did it.Timmy kicked me!"

Now little nurse Sara Jane's arrived,
clutching Sophie's hand.
"Sophie's got a tummy ache
and she doesn't want to stand."

No need to ask her why
with only crisps for lunch.
Sophie, pale and wan,
head down, shoulders hunched.

Tim just sits and watches.
He likes it in the corner pretending to read,
safe from the bigger bully boys
from whose clutches he's been freed.

James and John who've found a snail
come in to fetch a jar.
They say their mum is having twins
and dad's just bought a car.

Too soon they'll all come trooping back
to listen to *Monsters and More Gore*.
A few will have to practice reading
while their mothers gather, nattering by the door.

No regimental days here.
Play, work, love and understanding
and only the occasional Tim
needs reprimanding.

## THE AMSTERDAM

Drunken sailors beach ship
on maiden voyage just by Hastings -
seventeen hundred and forty nine.
Violent storm.

Two hundred and fifty years
salted in eight feet of mud and silt,
still three-quarters intact,
in fact, salvage-worthy for posterity.
Historic wreck must be saved.

Not by the Dutch who own it.
Not by the British so near it.
The Treasury reject it -
'Fifty metres too far south of coastal mean'
and the Dutch cannot get at it,
though they're keen.
'Conserve it!' cry the Archaeologists.
'Cover it with sand while we argue.'
A major bureaucratic row.

Twenty five million pounds,
give or take a hundred thousand,
the cost of rescue,
that decendants may know
how ancestors built ships.

She must be lifted,
washed and sifted,
deconstructed, reconstructed,
preserved in a museum
her artefacts laid bare,
her pickled wine declared,
as is the custom,
for all to view ad infinitum,

*if they know where to find the place*
*and can afford it*
*and have learned enough at their underfunded schools*
*with no textbooks or computers*
*or library.*

When the money is spent
and the great ship of great interest to everybody
is raised and displayed in ethereal splendour
it will be a wonderful thing.

For many generations to come
*someone* will say 'a job well done!'
and marvel at the workmanship,
the craftsmanship and shipmanship
and claim nostalgia for a time past.

*Those that know it's there,*
*wallowing in a museum.*
*Those that care it's there*
*preserved for posterity.*

## EAVESDROPPING
*(Cliff Path Walkers)*

They wander past below the house
not knowing that I'm there.
They talk of things I shouldn't hear
like money and the share
index and where to spend that million.

The lady with the woollen hat
and sturdy walking boots,
discusses bunions with her dog
then stoops to use the scoop,
flings muck towards the sea,
both verbal and otherwise,
saves her plastic bag.

Two runners shuffle past,
puffing and snorting through
the latest PB and ranking list
and how to combat nipple bleeding
or blisters and who should run
'The Seven Sisters'.

A pair of giggling lovers
find the secluded bench,
or so they hope,
and I learn a thing or two
about breasts and tits and flies
and other creatures that soar and swoop
and flit beneath the skies

until a gang of children,
wise to nature's ways,
fill the air with language
to set my ears ablaze.

## ANCESTORS

One line leads a century down from Cornwall
where granite-housed farmers
processed anchovies for Spain.
Another finds its way from Norway's Viking past,
an isolated farmstead by a fjord
where a swarthy Spanish sailor
left a sign in his descendants' hair.

A great, grand uncle on one side
left his mark in Bremen
- paintings in a German church,
and another composed a polka, or a waltz,
which I one day hope to play.

The grandfather who sang in stave church choirs,
sold sewing machines for 'Singer'
while his cousin sat in Parliament,
A grandmother on the other side,
whose father inspected steel ships in Japan,
nursed World War I soldiers.

Parents met in World War II.
He'd escaped from Nazis,
evaded quislings,
joined allied naval battles
on the rough Atlantic seas.
She'd laboured in her father's Essex fields
listening nightly for the doodlebugs.

# CHRISTMAS OUTSIDE HARRODS

Three youths huddle in a doorway
surrounded by some plastic bags trying,
on soggy bits of cardboard, to convey
some hopeless message.
Fur coats dangle in a glazed display,
tinsel-decked and mocking,
while a man swathed in white sheets
flaps by, sandalled in the rain,
cloth sack soaking, and an old woman
in three woolly hats, sits silently
holding her stomach; rocking.

## THE DISMANTLING OF THE HOTEL

Green corrugated underlay
lies tossed in a twisted heap.
Faded, deep-pile carpet,
under-vacuumed and also green,
blocks an entrance.
A smart receptionist smiled there once;
greeted salesmen and newlyweds.

Wood-lice and frustrated spiders
trundle and scurry from beneath
piles of torn flocked wallpaper,
no longer wine and gold.

Light fittings, bared electric flex,
copper piping, tank lagging,
and broken ceiling tiles,
- polystyrene of course,
as favoured in the 70's,
are flung out without ceremony through
the only unboarded window.

All unfitted furniture went last week
leaving one teak-effect 60's table,
coffee stained, veneer blistered,
to soak up the drizzle.

Dust covered dismantlers whistle and guffaw;
something they find in a bottom drawer.

The 50's hotel is going
piece by piece by piece.
It will be dust next week.
Vacant building plot.
New home for a new lot!

## CHANCING LUCK

Chancing luck we made a syndicated guess
and joined the weekly gamble in the press.
We'd hoped to win a prize of many pounds
to sweep and rake and place in bounteous mounds
before our mentors - seeking to impress.

With care we entered names and home address
and checked and double-checked our forms no less
than twenty times; for accuracy abounds,
chancing luck.

So, holding on to dreams in hopefulness,
with bated breath we waited, but confess,
our hearts went racing freely with the hounds.
There were no cheers, just tears and whimpering sounds
when all was lost. But then we sought redress -
chancing luck.

## ALICE IS STAYING

I'm not going, not going
horn blowing, horn blowing,
she said.
She sat in bed
wrapped in crumpled sheets
wrapped in sheets.

Corn mowing did you say?
I want to play, want to play.
She tapped her spoon,
spilt her porridge,
tapped her spoon.

What a day, what a day!
And who are you?
My son you say.
Just go away, go away!
I'm Alice.

## THE REUNION

You met me there beside the fallow land,
sometime between the cock-crow and high noon.
My daughter's daughter held your filial hand.

Your smiling face brought back the harvest moon
when ripening ricks of corn, like shadows, stood
to guard my sleep while papa hummed a tune.

Your flaxen hair, the haystack by the wood
which surrounded the old tree-house uncle built.
He joined a war I never understood.

Those eyes; my eyes, pooled innocence and guilt,
showed clear the day my sister wed her beau
and I hid the legless spider in her quilt!

I saw me there as you will never know.
I met again myself in your small frame.
All the years between us seemed to flow

down the winding path to Jack's Millstream.
That's where I found the frogspawn and the fish
and caught the lovers napping in their dream.

Your voice; my voice, soft spoke a simple wish
that we could stay forever there to play
and share the bread and dripping from my dish.

But your mother took your hand away.
"He's old," she said, "His mind's begun to stray."

# FORGET YESTERDAY?

Forties born and fifties bred,
sixties reared and fed and bled.
Pills and sex and sixty-nine,
hairbands, beards and beads on string.

You say I should forget all that?
Forget the dreams?
The torn worn jeans. The third world dress,
kaftans, sandals - Jesus' style,
coarse red wine and pot and grass,
guitar strumming in the park
and singing 'anti' songs?

We could make love then and forget
ourselves. Sod tomorrow.

And that was wrong, you say?
Today, be careful of the kissing,
use a condom, don't share needles,
no need for sex, it's in the bottle.

Yesterday has gone, man.
Yesterday has gone?

## RUNNER'S CAPSULE

For you sifters of the future, I leave this little capsule.
It is token-filled and bulging, for in running
I'm indulging, and I think you'll find surprise
in what we use for exercise circa 1996:-

One pair *NikeAir* waffle-soled trainers - size 5.
One stop-watch, time zoned international
with built-in monitor for heart-rate
giving lap times which are fractional.

A pair of thermal duofold gloves.
A tub of yellow jelly vaseline,
plus blister kit with 'second skin'.
One *Heli* long-sleeved vest, fleece lined.

A reflective bib and two armbands.
One *KnightLite* - ultra-bright
with long life batteries
*Ever-Ready* and ultra-light.

A plastic waist pouch and bottle belt
with pocket key and coin holder.
A diet sheet with calendar
and work-out book in plastic folder.

A mini receiver with headphones.
One pair 1000 mile socks in blue.
One full sponsor sheet for charity
- pledges for collection by 2002.

One pair lycra speed-shorts
in cerise and lime with matching vest.
One 'Sub-4 Atlanta' motif Tee-shirt
embroidered and embossed.

A Vortex (hydrophilic membrane system) waterproof.
One video with excerpts from great races:
'The Three Peaks', 'The Seven Sisters',
some mountains in Wales during force 8 gales.

One *Hi-Five* isotonic drink in silver-foil bag.
A packet of *Green Essence* powdered
'Salad-in-a-glass' with fourteen
vegetables and four healthy herbs.

One box of *Breathe-Right* nose strips
with extra strong adhesive grip
plus one superweave paper tissue
for catching that elusive drip.

One pair *Sorbothane* insoles -
extra light with orthotic wedged heel.
One 'minimum-bounce' sports bra
with not an ounce of sex appeal.

One Ron Hill publication entitled
'The Long Hard Road - Book 2'
One tin deep heat muscle rub.
One shoe repair kit with tube of super-glue.

An assortment of luminous laces.
A wrist-band with handy zip.
One display box with medals.
One London Marathon rejection slip.

# NEXT DOOR

Time moves on.

The neighbours are building a house;
A bungalow, in granite,
With pool and double garage,
And landscaped gardens.

Our house is disintegrating.
Paint peels from the window frames,
Loose tiles shudder in the wind,
Weeds fill the flower beds.

The 'house next door' rises
From old ruins, takes on a new life
With new gates, solid rock walls,
And a fresh black tarmac driveway.

Our house just gets more dull,
More grey with each passing day.
Now we're the ones 'next door'
With a house in need of more
Than just a touch of paint

## REFLECTIONS ON MR. GOHEEN

Old man Goheen has gone now,
he followed the death of his job.
Retired from the railroad maintenance gang.
. . . Well, he was more than sixty five,
and it was the work kept him alive.
No shirking from his duties,
hovering, crone-like, over his hammer,
driving in the spikes,
repairing lines for diesels.
His workmates watched over him,
watched under, round and back of him,
as he shovelled up the gravel
in the mosquito heat,
or frozen January.
Never stripped to the navel
like his mates.
No bare-chested bravado for him.
Just a good day's work for a good day's pay.

## 62 BAYSWATER ROAD W2
*(Secretarial College 1964/65)*

A few years ago,
I learned to touch-type at some college.
A hundred thousand times
I typed repeated lines
about coming to the aid of the party -
I never did learn whose.

I wondered who the good men were.
Perhaps they'd been the good boys;
the ones who deserved the food
from the scales of *egbdf.*
Let's *face* it, I still have trouble
reading music; but I can type.

And then I learned some shorthand
using squiggles, dots and dashes,
so lost the art of writing.
Couldn't get words down fast enough,
still can't, so now I *have* to type.

## KISSING THE MOBILE PHONE

Saw her white teeth flash
as she hurtled past
one hand upon the wheel.

Saw her smart car swerve
when it bumped the curb;
action-replay, strange, surreal.

Saw her keep that smile
on her face for a while,
as though she could not feel

she was there alone
with her mobile phone
in her coffin of crumpled steel.

## MOON CLOWN

He's only a clown from some Eastern state
who carries his past on a shattered plate.
There's a spring in his step, a swing in his gait,
and his pink pantaloons always seem to inflate
to his sober tune.

But, give him a song and some coarse red wine,
he'll lurch and he'll trip and he'll hunch up his spine
like a wandering tramp by a railway line,
with his oversized shoes and frayed belt of twine,
for he's not immune

to the cries of his fellows who fell before;
who found themselves on the wrong side of a war.
No - there's paint on his face to cover much more
than the pain of the wounds that he stoically bore
and his heart's a balloon.

It swells and it bursts as he frolics along
playing the fool to a gathering throng,
playing for laughs to some crowd for a song,
wondering if he can ever belong
under that clown of a moon.

## A ROOM IN OUR HOUSE

There is a sign on the bedroom door
'Personal! Private! Keep Out!'
I open it anyway
to place the ironed, folded clothes
neatly on a chair.
My eyes scan the forbidden room,
the unmade bed, the den, the gloom,
then I stoop to pick up soiled socks,
discarded underclothes, a crumpled skirt.
There is another sign
'Trespassers must pay a fine!
Place 5p in this tin'
I reach deep into my pocket,
fumble for a coin,
and grudgingly pop it in.

## JUNGLE OF JOISTS

What will it look like,
the new house,
when the last ridge-tile is placed;
the last brick pointed?

A jungle of joists now,
I watch the builders
hoist the frames, peg the felt
I hear them hammer,
crack stone against stone,
scrape cement into cavities,
trundle barrows over gravel.

When they've finished,
how strange the place will be,
bereft of bobble hats,
'time of day' banter,
bleeping pagers,
plaster dust and navvy brawn.

How strange without the music,
without the radio cackle,
when silence re-asserts itself
over the new laid lawn.

## FAMILY ARCHIVES
*(Through the Looking Glass)*

This is where I hope to find
the reason why my eyes are blue,
why my hair is tangled blonde,
my dappled skin - a ruddy hue.

Which donor dealt the tantrum,
which one the double chin,
who's to blame for the knobbly knees,
and the crooked 'Cheshire' grin?

This nose - a bulbous after-thought,
these hands so cracked and dry,
which forbear had the vision
to pass on this wandering eye?

And if like the 'Still' photographer,
I could re-touch and enhance,
would my mirrored critic
still give me such a glance?

## CHANGING LIFE AT ELY
*(Autumn 1963)*

Through the station at Ely,
on the flat of the fens
I felt my first loss
of a time, which till then,
had been mine.
There on the flat,
flat over flat
flat to the Isle of Ely,
tracking a line
between the cathedrals
watching for spires
spiking the cloak
of a fast changing sky,
I stifled my cry.
How could I explain
my thoughts on that train
as it swayed its slow way
through the fens?
There's no place, I'd found,
so bleak and forlorn,
no place so eerie and wild.
But some mystical muses
have slyly conspired,
have tricked out a beauty
so subtle,
I feel a strange longing
remembering that train
that bore me so slowly
through Ely.

# SHOWING THE WAY

One day I'll show her how to iron
and fold and stow her clothes -
but not just yet.
I'll let her childhood play awhile.
Perhaps the right time will be
when she comes to me
and asks if that huge pile,
that stacked-up-heap of clothing,
needs attention.
That's when I'll mention
how I earned my first day's wage
ironing clothes for neighbours,
the ones with seven children.
She'll look at me all-knowing then,
as though she's heard it all before.

## SEASON'S GREETINGS

Rushing to the shops
no-one ever stops
to reason

while filling plastic bags
with gifts and wraps and tags
of the season.

They'll get what they want
never mind the cost,
there is good reason,

and they'll have sauce with turkey
this Christmas, most surely,
for they have the spirit to seize on.

That pivotal day

when I baked my own fruit cake,
dusted off much cluttered shelves,
rearranged treasured trinkets,
made ready the silent room.

When the *almost* strangers gathered
to greet or kiss or shake hands
and retied the loosened strings
back around the family package.

When familiar voices filled the place
with half forgotten anecdotes,
rekindled spent arguments
and reworded filial gossip.

When we feasted on *then* and *those* days,
drank toasts to *tomorrow* and *always*
until the party ended with the cake ablaze
and fifty burning candles turned to smoke.

## A CANADIAN EXPERIENCE

Fossilized driftwood by sitka-lined lakes.
Bears flipping salmon in the cool of some falls.
A wolf's chilling howl on a clear winter night.
Migrating geese, high in their arrow-head flight.
Power-saws screaming through primeval forests.
Diesel trains humming up snaking steel lines.
Blueberry picking for blueberry pie,
and

aurora borealis.

## INVENTION AND A SOFT TOUCH

In dealing with invention
it is my intention to discuss
the connection between man
and his need, or his greed.

Innovation, it seems,
feeds not only on necessity,
and man, being blessed with tenacity,
can make good use of his brain facility
to get what he wants.
But he's not alone. Indeed,

let's compare the blackbird with the snail
impaled on his beak. One knock
on a rock and the contents are freed.
Or the otter who lies back on his bed of sea,
cracking clams with a stone,
- invention out of need,

with my cat,
fat and overfed,
who rubs up my leg to beg
for the little bit of skate left on my plate
and gets it
- invention out of greed.

## SEEDLESS GRAPE

On the vine a ripened grape -
so plump and cool and green,
so promising of sweetness.

Pluck it from its over-laden host
and bring it to your waiting lips.

Draw it in to the cavern of your mouth.
Wrap and squeeze with testing tongue;
free fresh juice and let it run
slowly, coolly down your throat.

Clasp the broken fruit in the pincer of your hand.
Trap the bitter skin between your teeth.
Twist and roll with eager tongue;
expose the veined and jellied flesh beneath.

. . . press that flesh; sweet, so sweet,
to the roof of your mouth.

## CASTING SHADOWS

I caught them casting shadows on a screen,
their slim and nimble fingers intertwined.
They giggled with delight at every shape
that conjured up a new suggestive sign.
Innocence went slipping from the scene.

I caught them casting shadows on the wall,
their slim and nimble bodies interlocked.
They sighed with loving pleasures, I recall,
as their convoluted shadows gently rocked.
I switched the master light off in the hall.

## TODAY I'M FEELING FAT

The keep-fit class is full of fit young blondes.
I'm sure that none are half as fat as me.
They kick and stretch their long and slender legs
Without a sign of pain in hip or knee.

Their lithe and supple bodies bend and sway
In bright and sexy skin-tight leotards
That squeezed on me just emphasize the lumps.
I think I'll quit and take to playing cards!

## EXTRA CURRICULAR ACTIVITIES

I'm waiting in the rain again,
seated in my foggy-windowed car
in the vandal-tainted car-park
by the school.
This is my second home
where children's detritus,
like sticky toffee wrappers
and notes of great importance
from the P.T.A.,
wallow in a sea of khaki
game's-field mud.
It's here in this fish-tank
cover for a front room
that I ponder away the hours
willing the match to finish
or the dancing lesson to end.

## BOOTING UP

Too much is said
about the World Wide Web.
It seems to be the new God.
All party talk is of connections
each new convert knows-it-all.
Computer literati -
“Oh yes, we have a Modem.
We are the history makers.
It’s a mystery more don’t interact
with time compressed and space compact.”

It’s like the third dimension
alluded to in 50’s sci-fi.
We open up the dull grey window
framed in dull grey plastic,
peer into a void;
order words; submit codes;
then pass through
to Honolulu, Helsinki, Kathmandu.
We ride on waves of space
exploring, searching, finding,
until someone sneezes,
connections crash
and the window’s closed.